The ABC's of Luxury

BY PrettyG and Jeff Dec

This book was designed by us to excite, motivate, and help young minds be as creative as possible. Teaching the alphabet or number counting was the only educational concept included in most coloring books of my era. With "The ABC's of Luxury" we are trying to open up a new lane of interest to children of all ages. As a child some of our favorite forms of expressions were to draw our favorite sneakers or the logos of our favorite cars.. With the impact of the internet on today's youth, kids know more about luxury brands than ever before, so we decided to give them apart of the high end lifestyle and let their artistic creativity bringing their own ideas to life. Helping the youth understand that other individuals had a vision and brought that vision to life, and they can do the same. We hope the brands and designs featured in the book not only offer a fun way of learning but open up the opportunity to bring parents and children together. It was our mission to help bridge the gap between all ages and bring something exciting and fun to families.

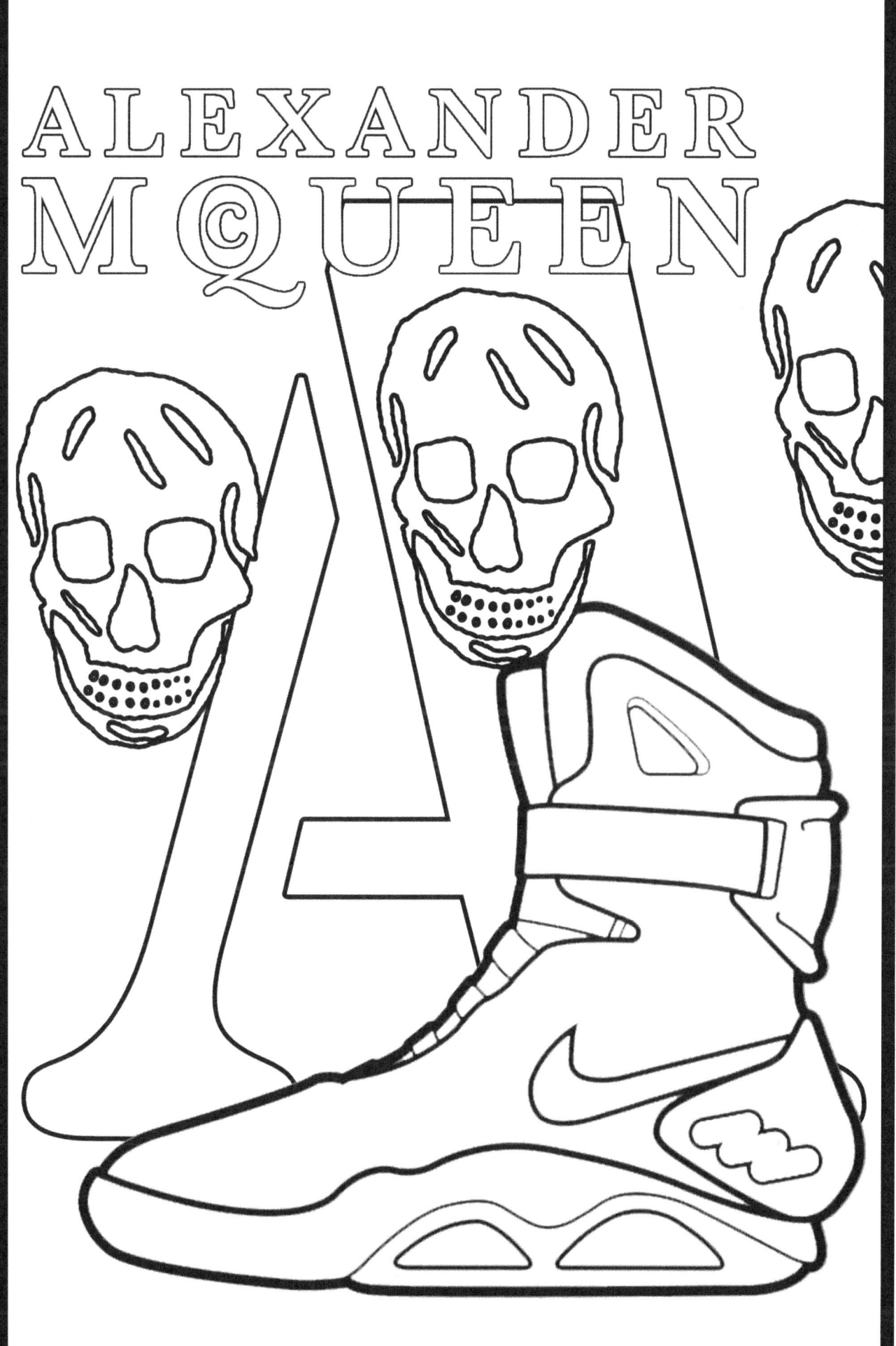

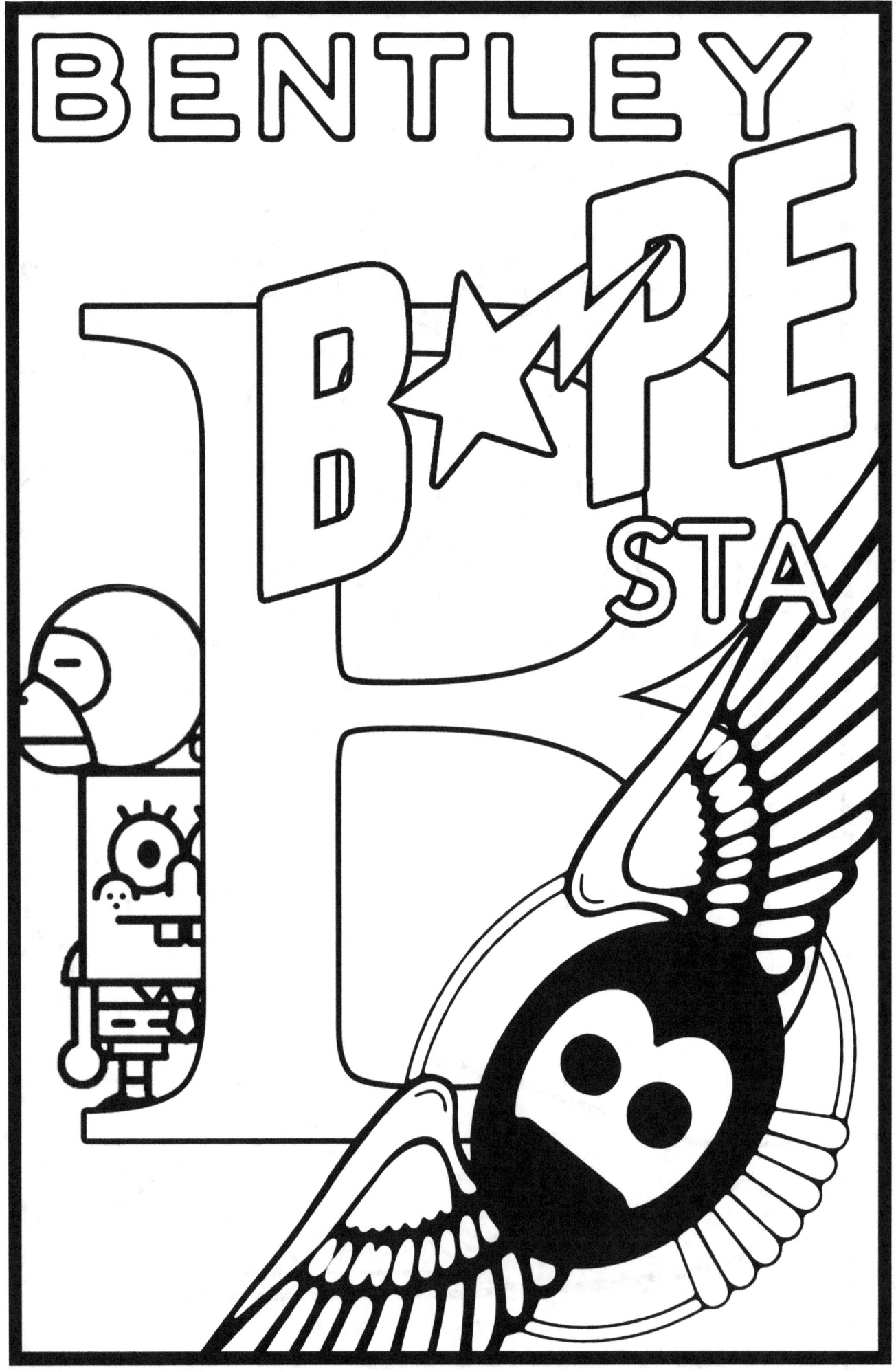

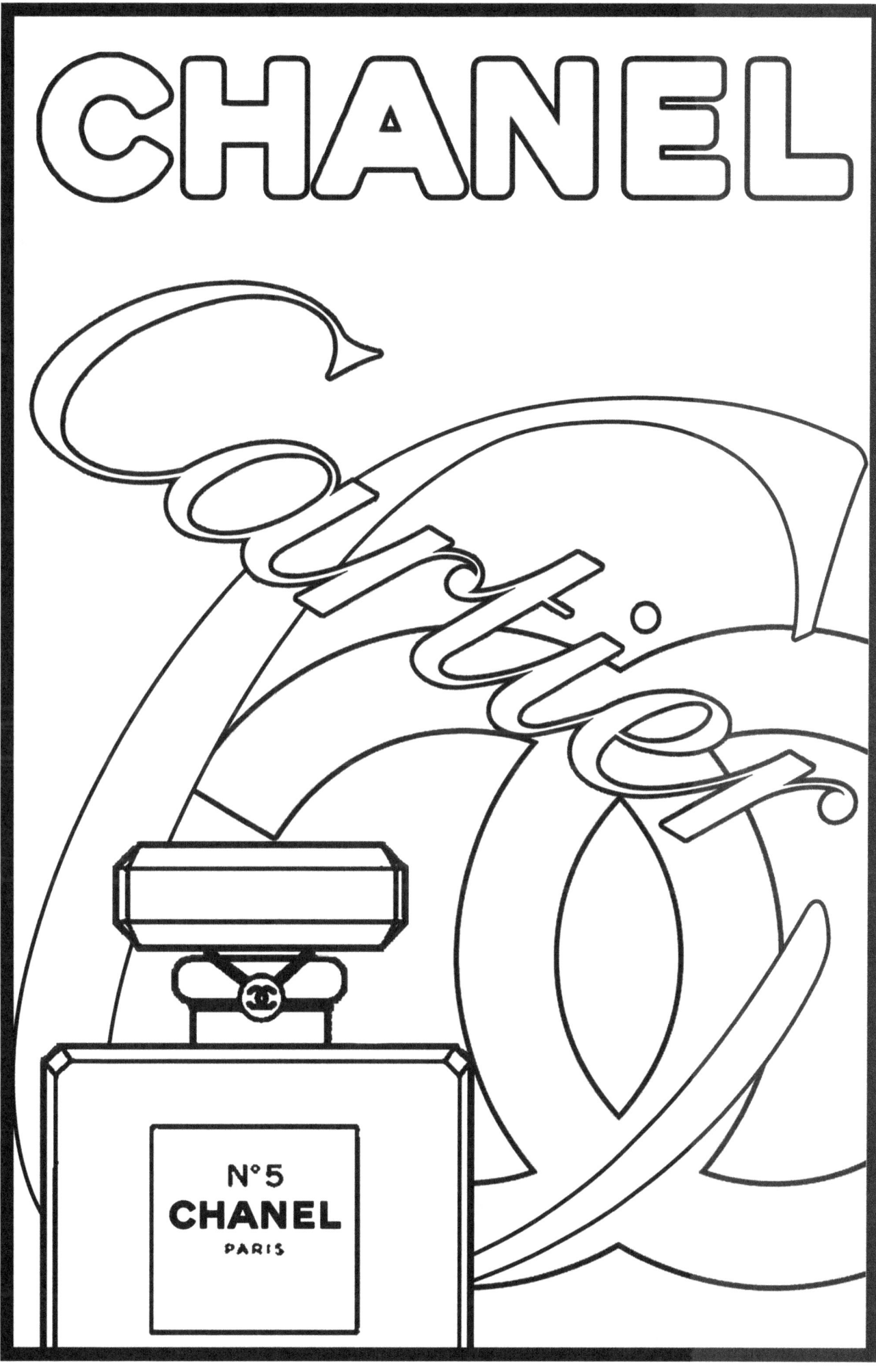

DOLCE & GABBANA

Christian Dior

Dior

D&G

Dapper Dan

EMILIO PUCCI

Ed Hardy ®
By Christian Audigier

LOVE KILLS SLOWLY

FENDI

ferrari

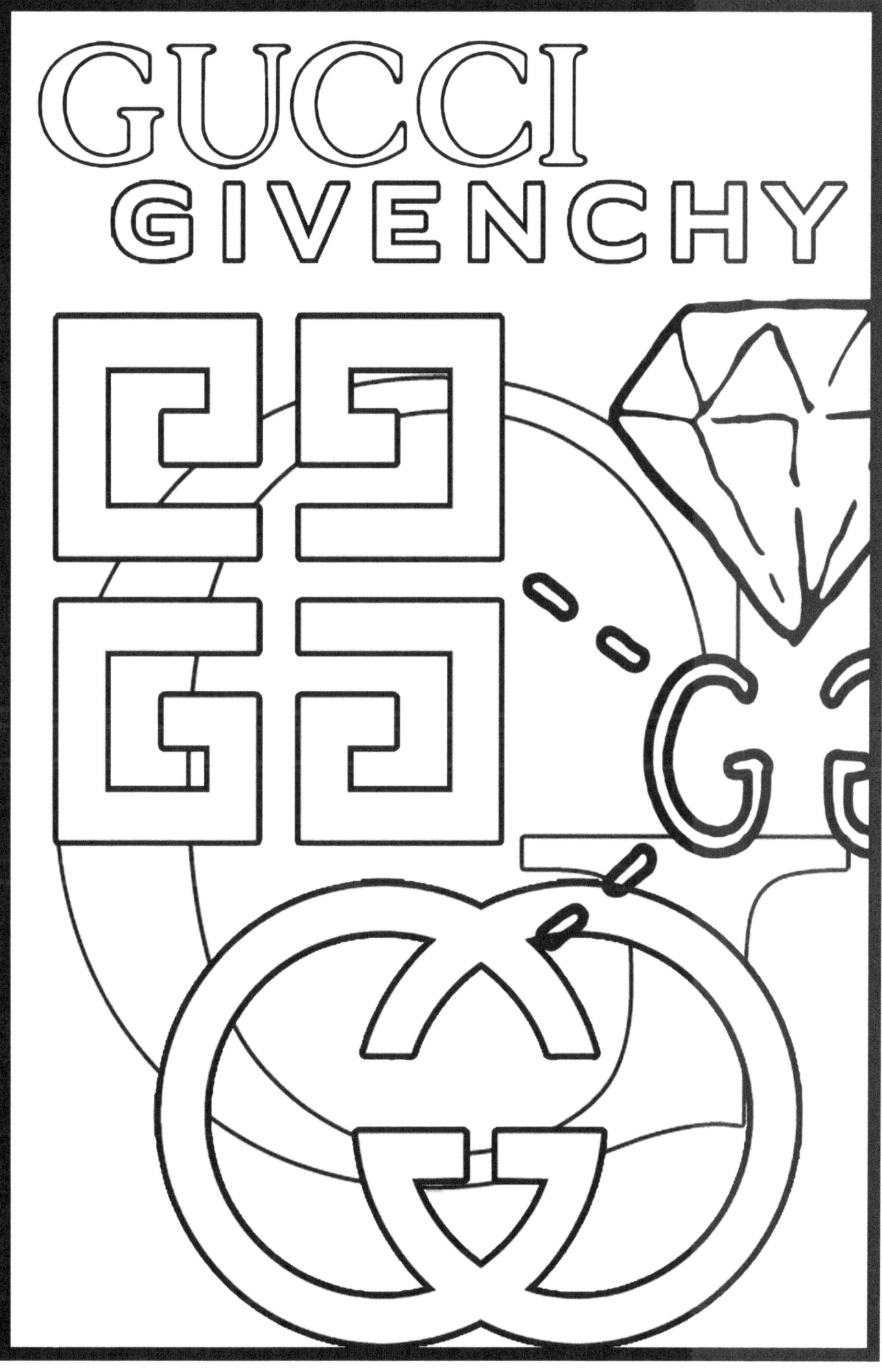

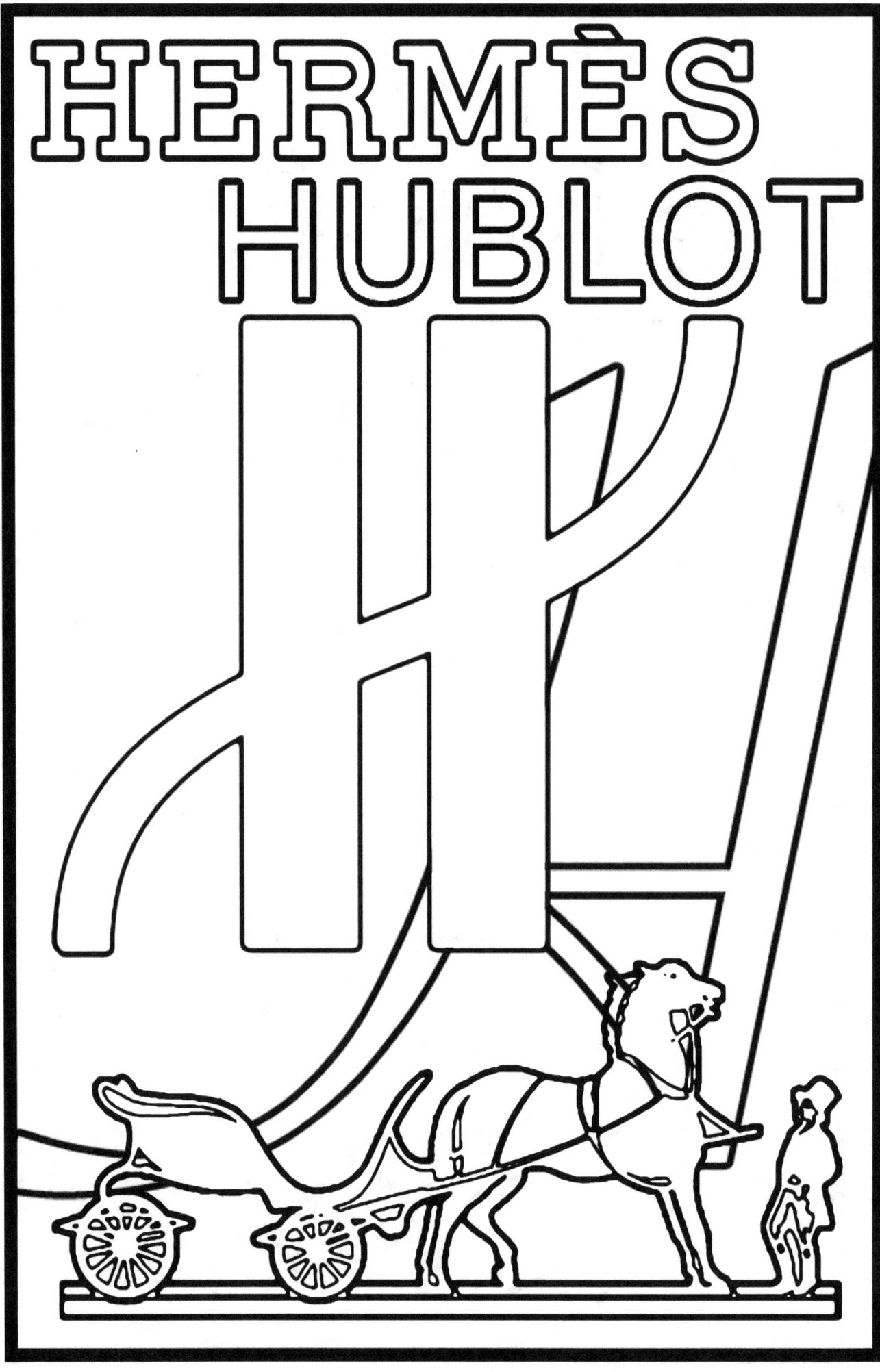

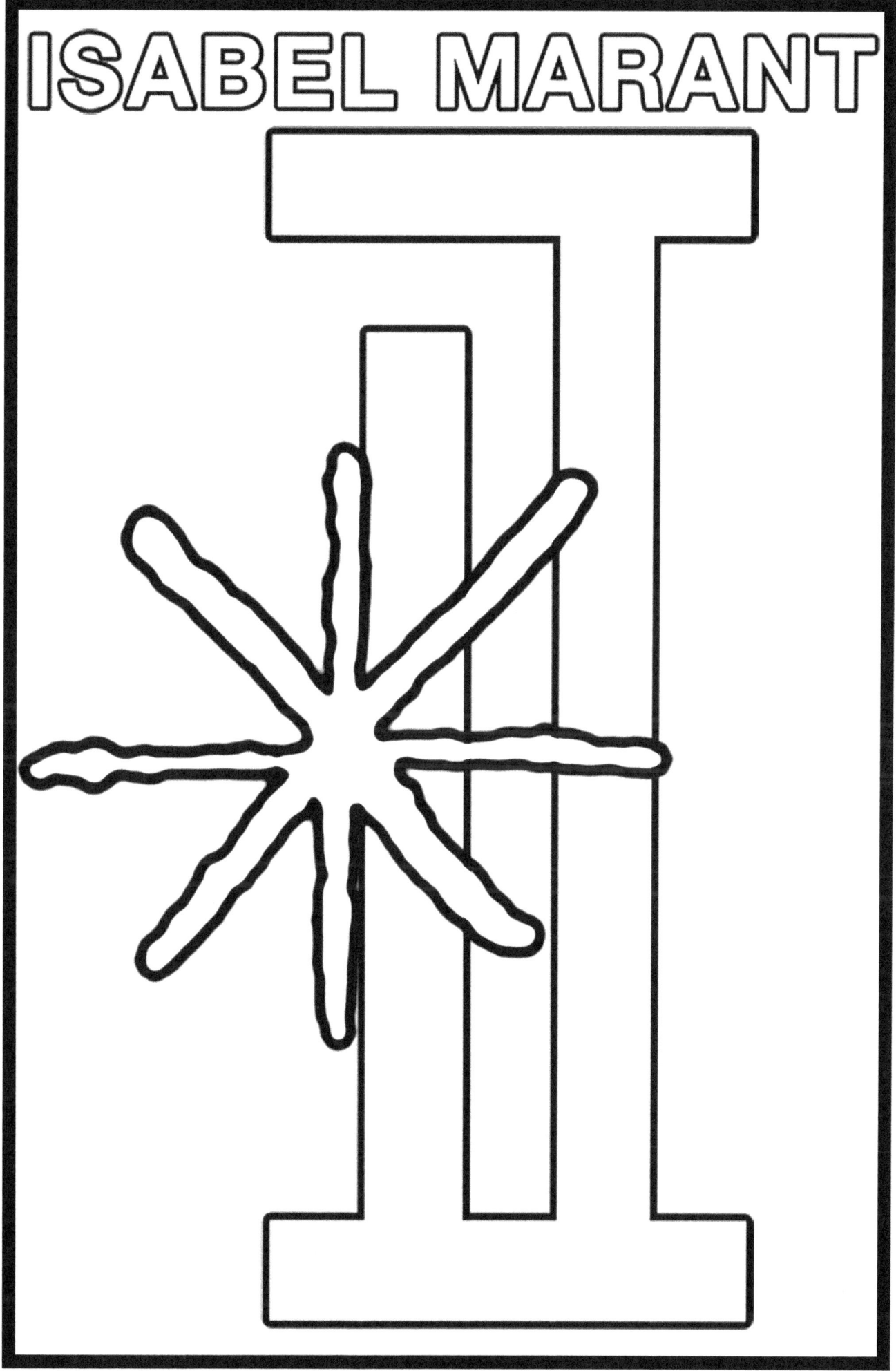

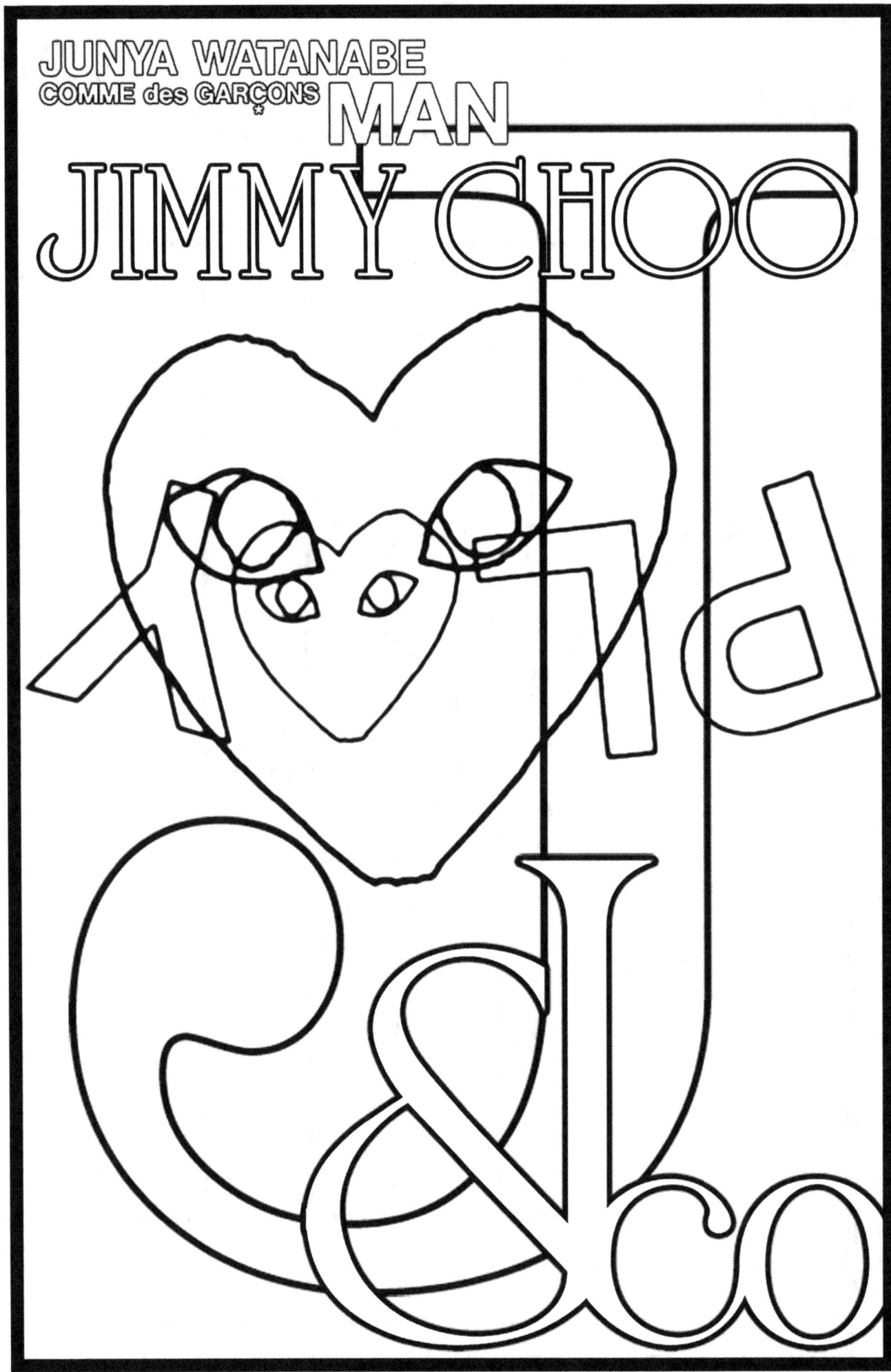

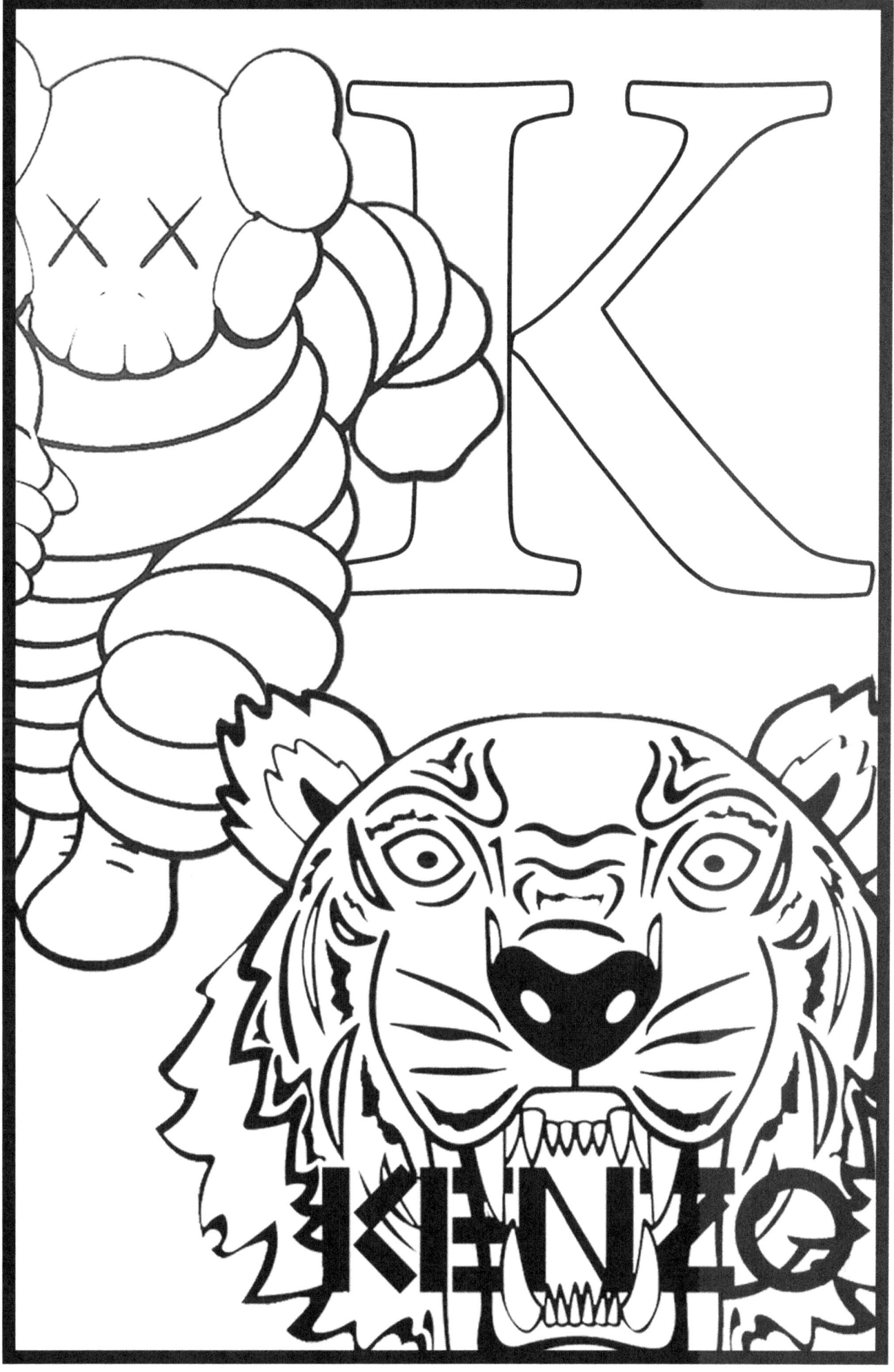

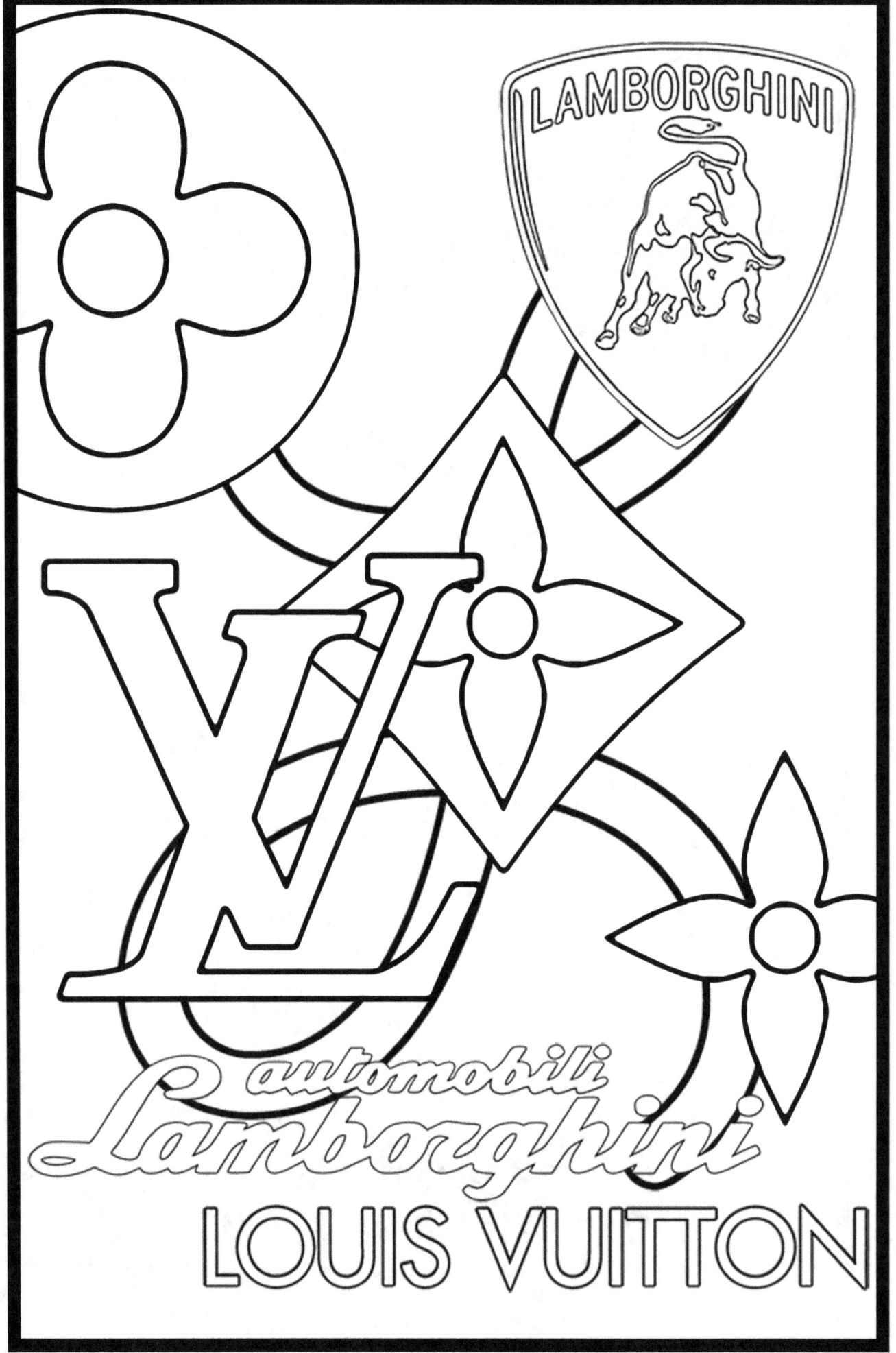

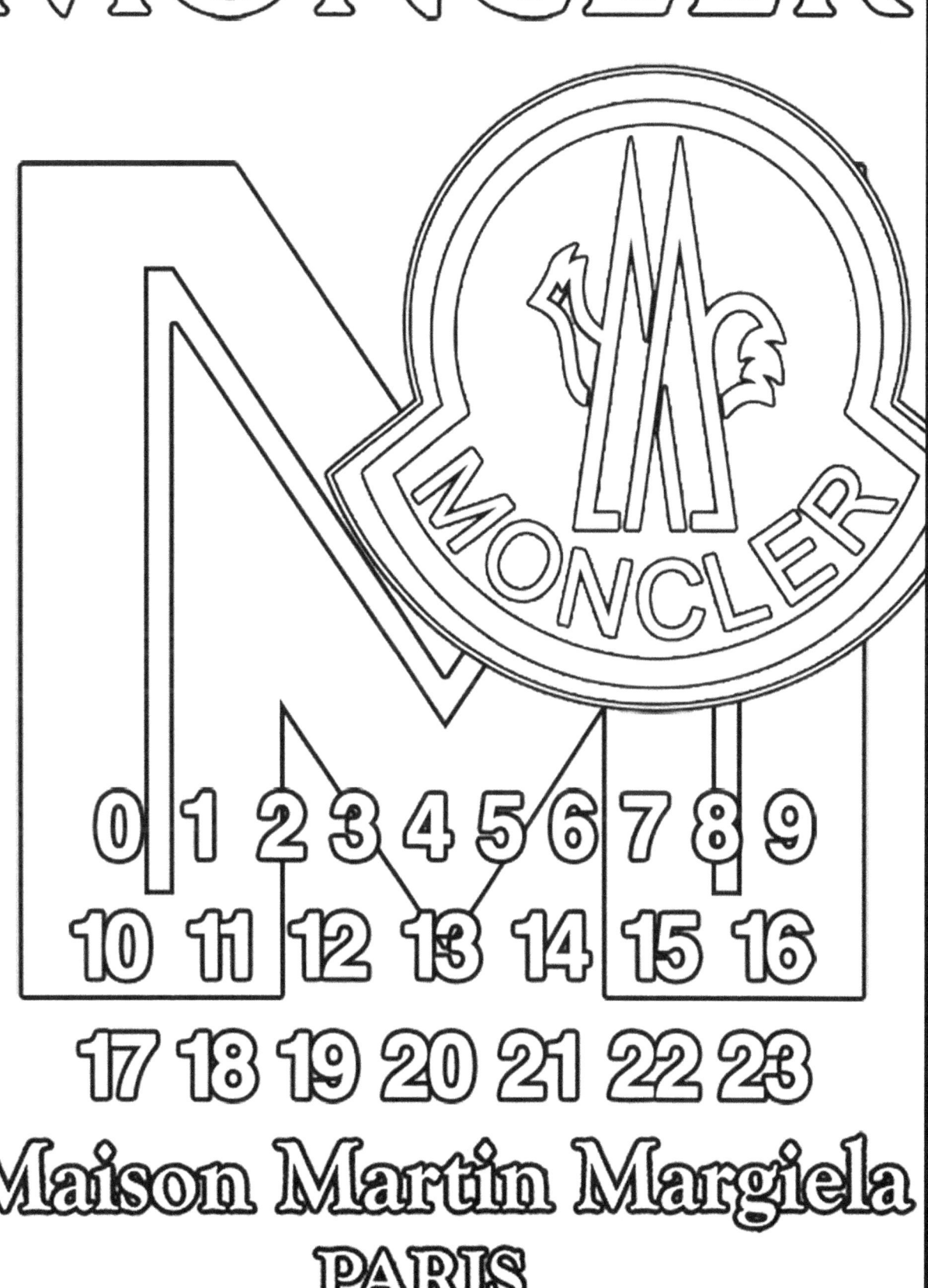

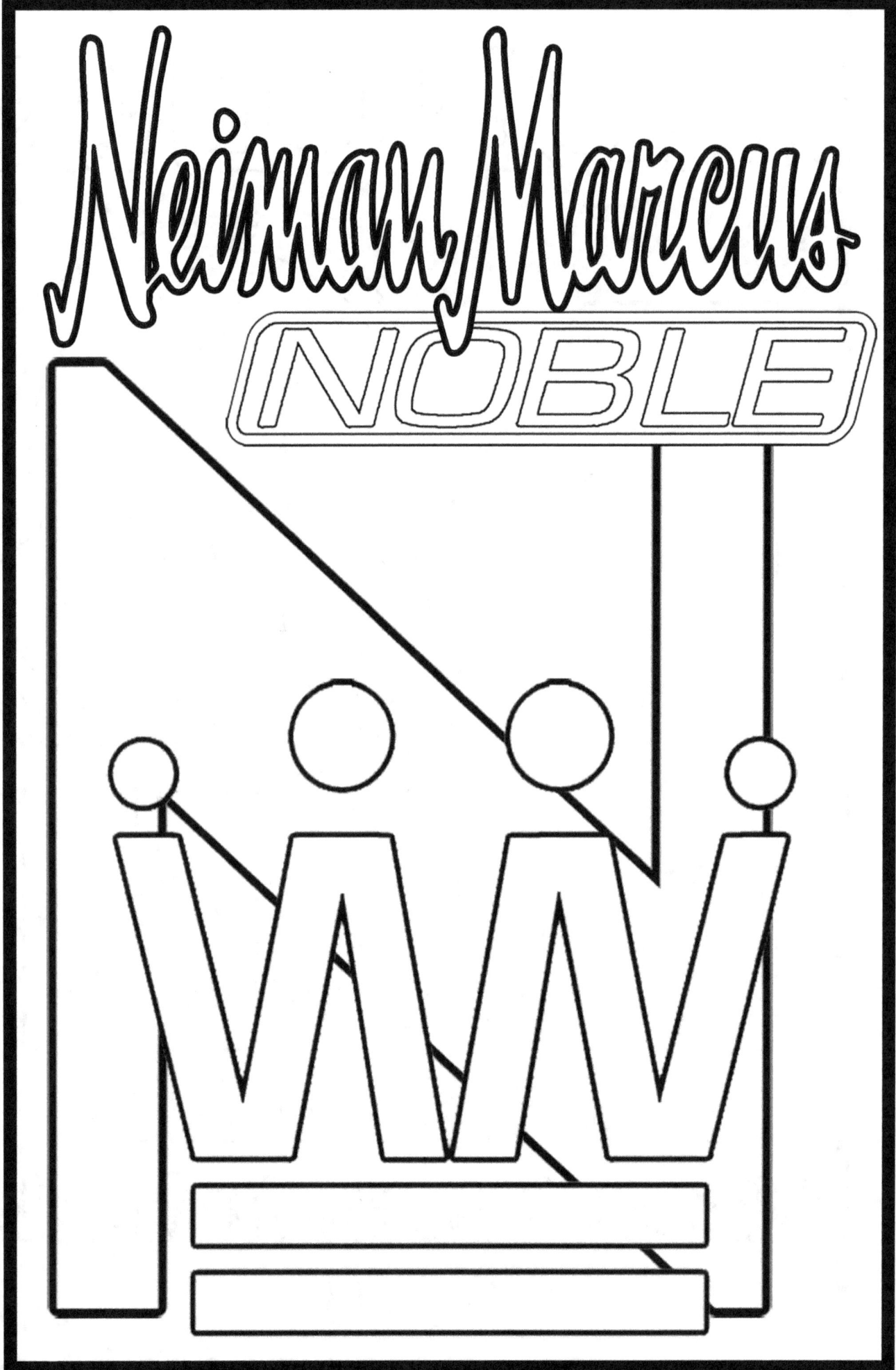

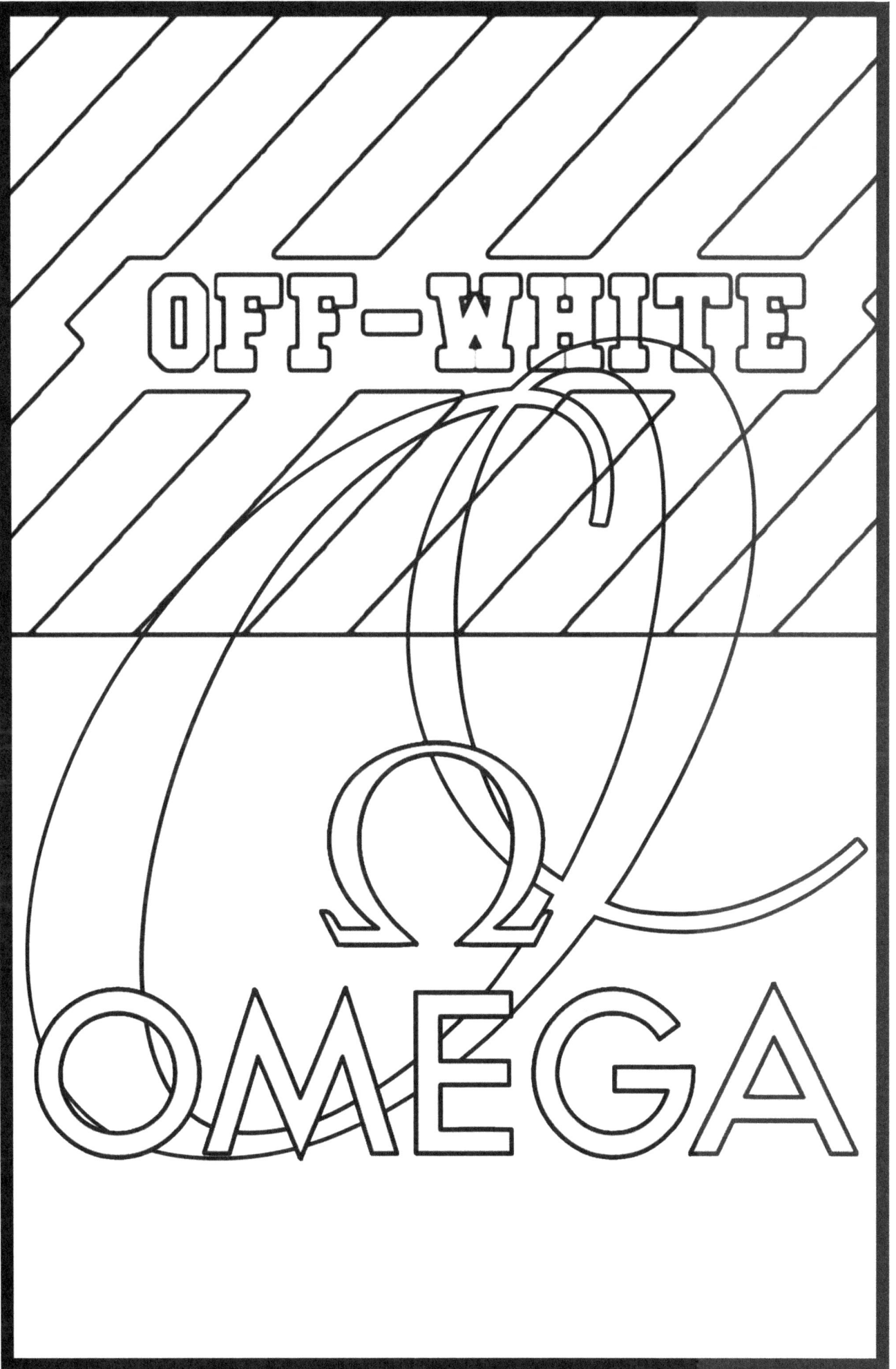

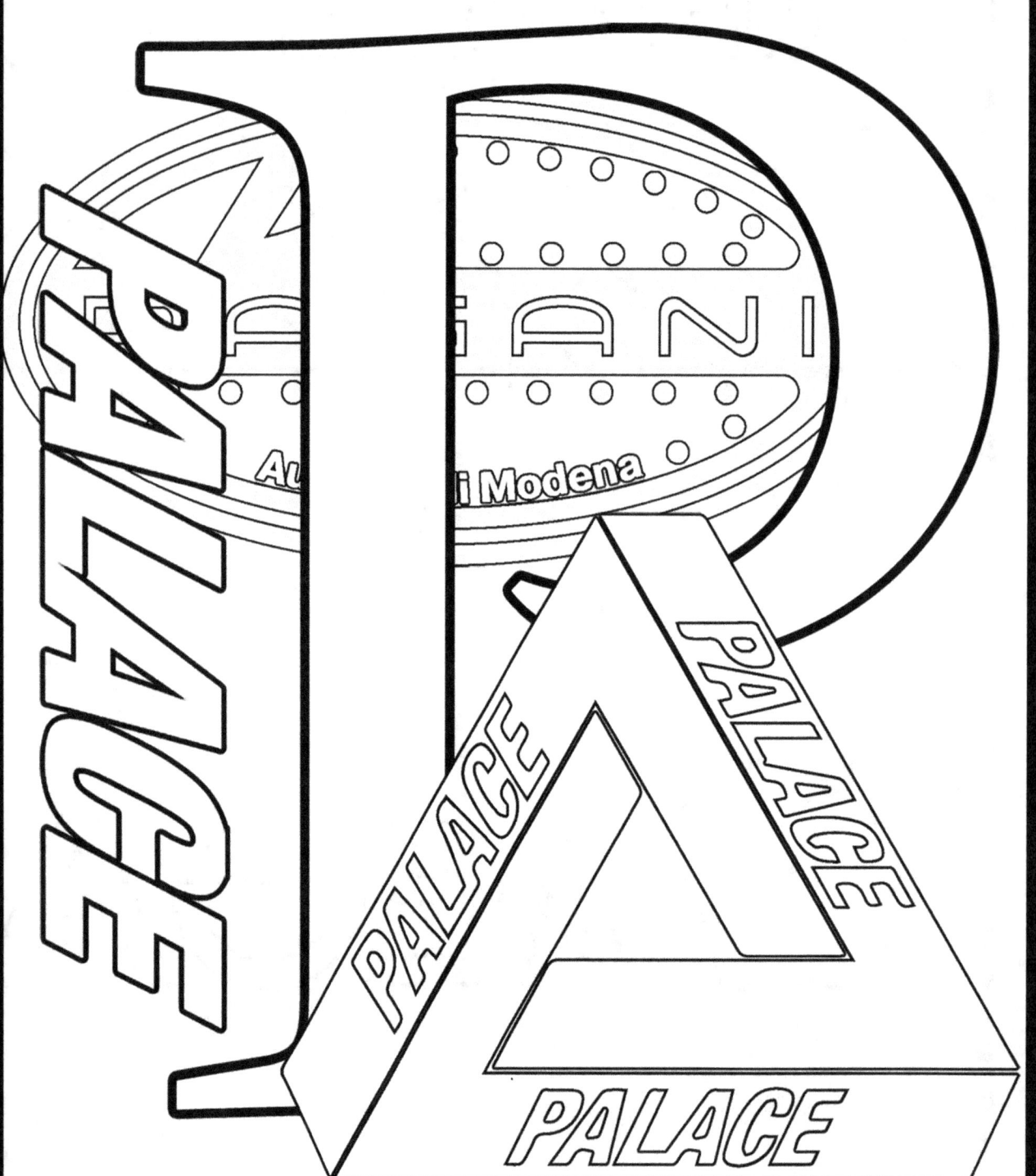

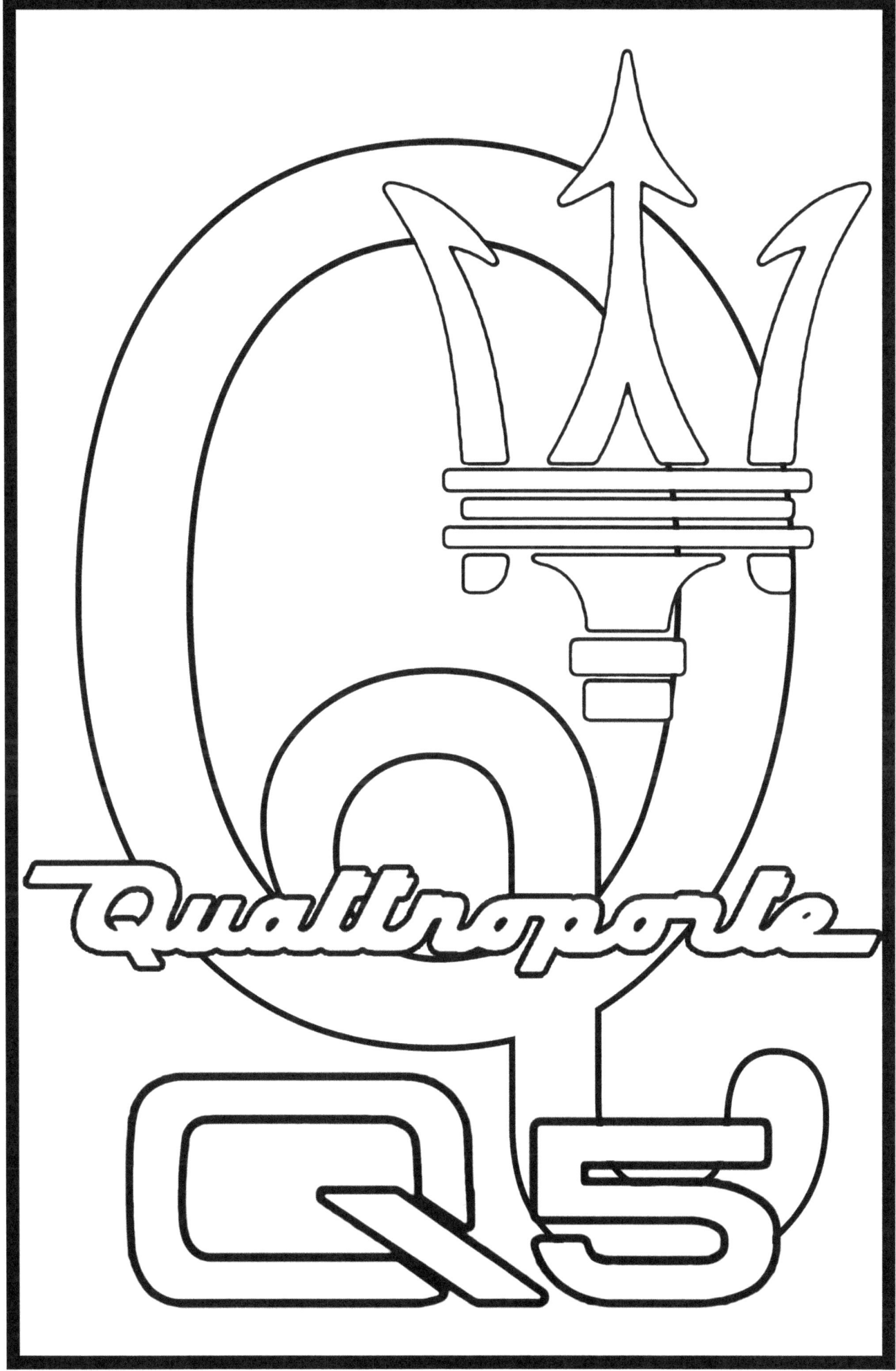

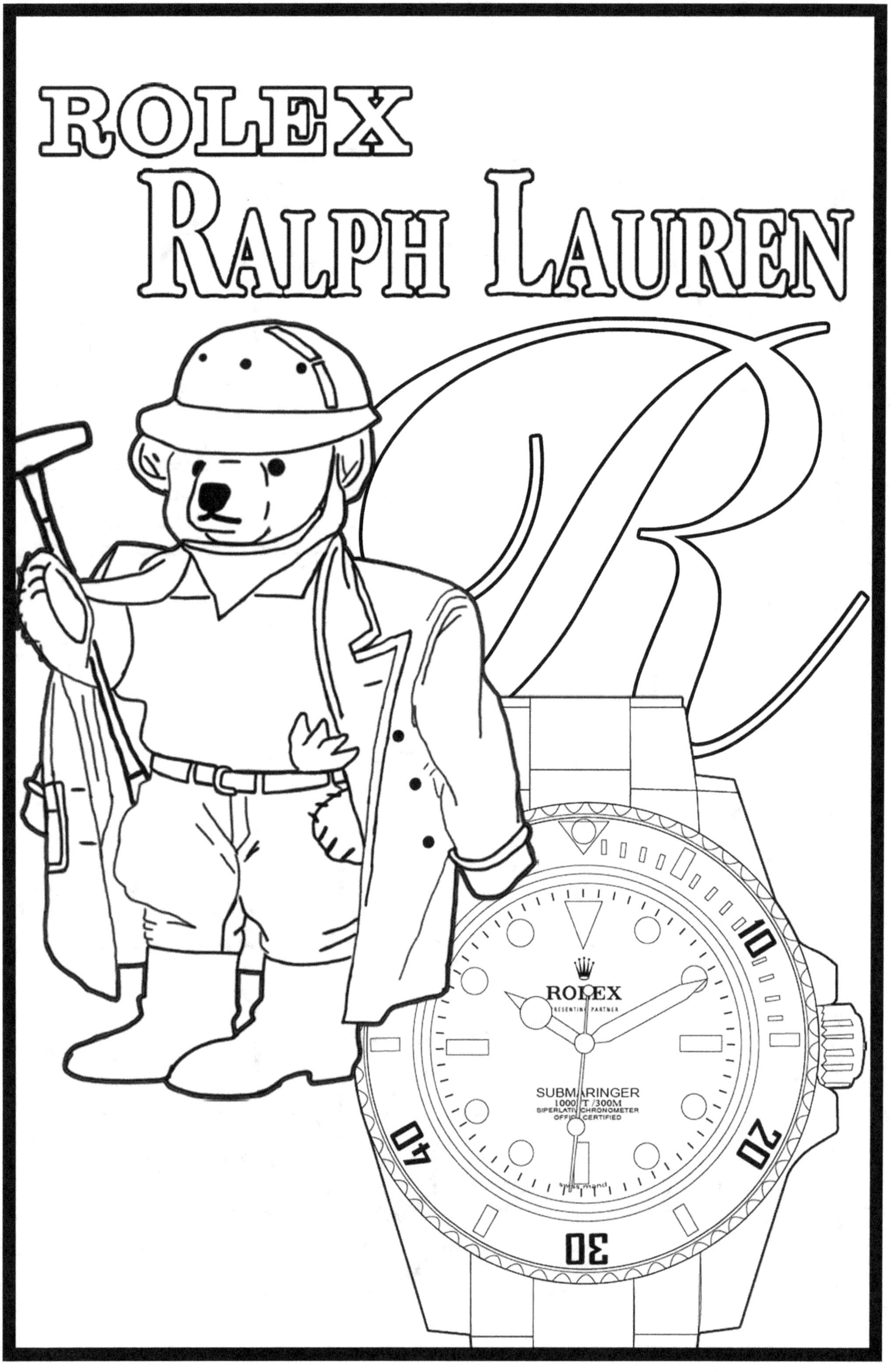
ROLEX
RALPH LAUREN
ROLEX
SUBMARINGER
10
20
30
40

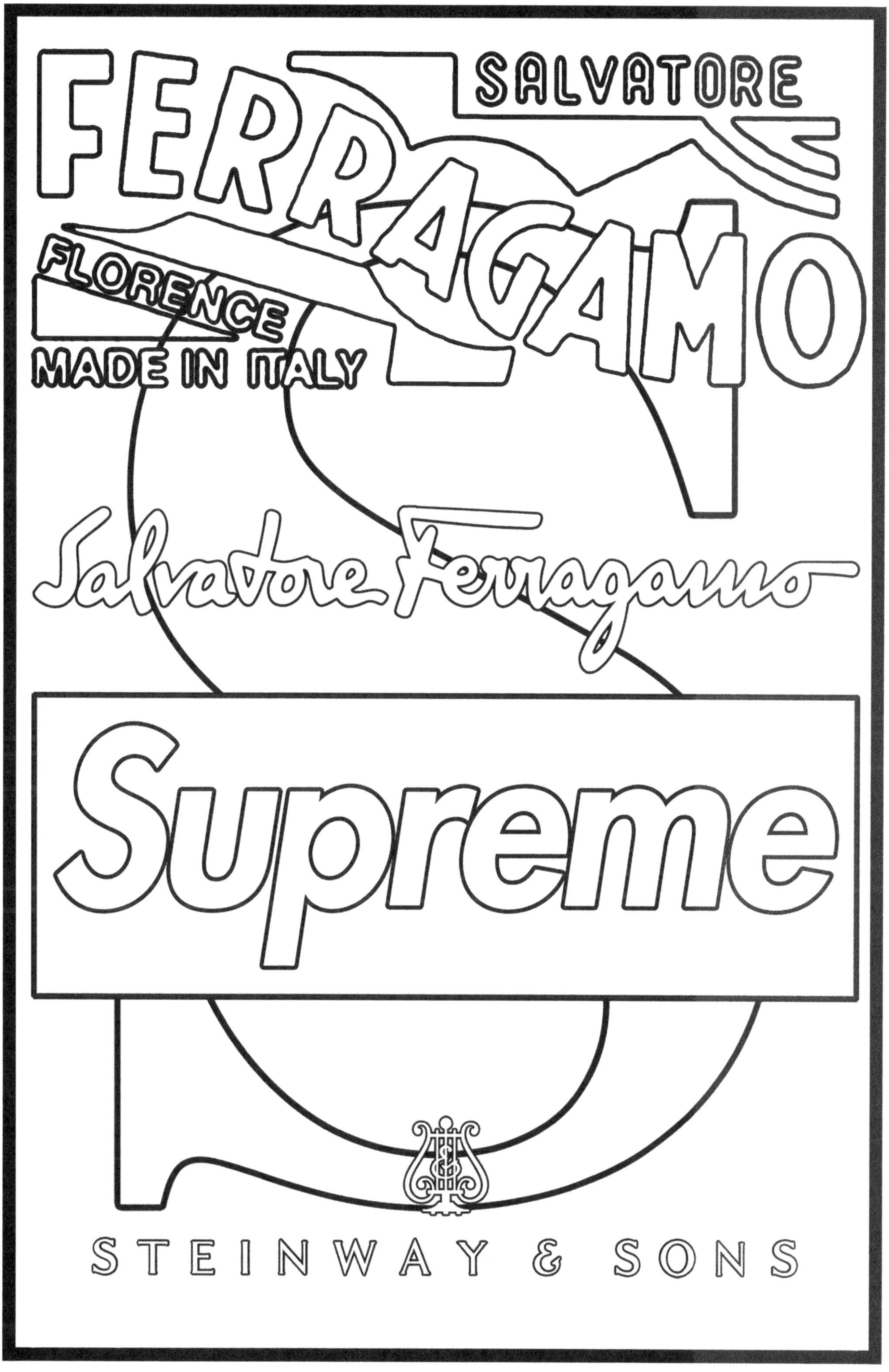
SALVATORE
FERRAGAMO
FLORENCE
MADE IN ITALY
Salvatore Ferragamo
Supreme
STEINWAY & SONS

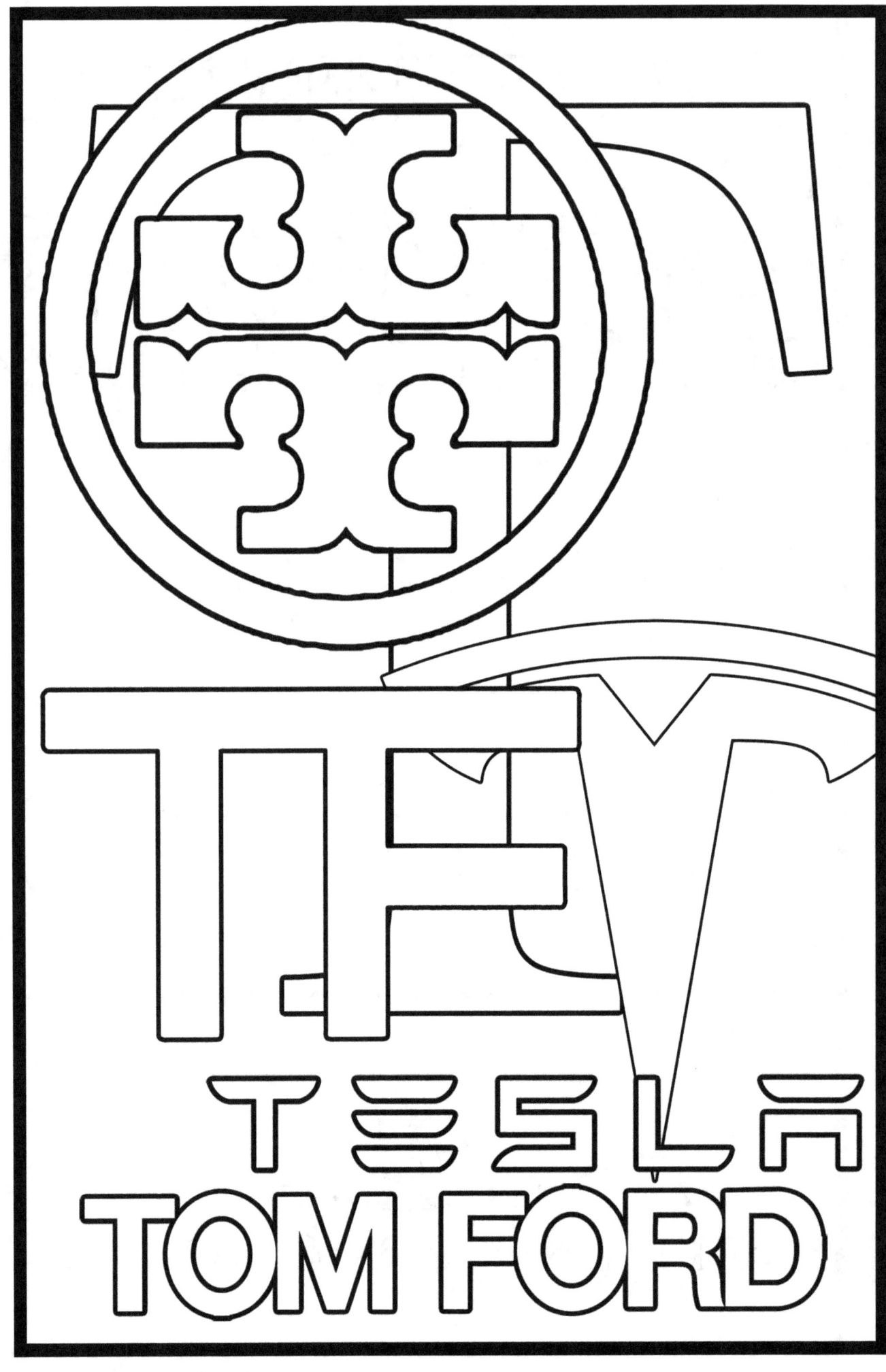

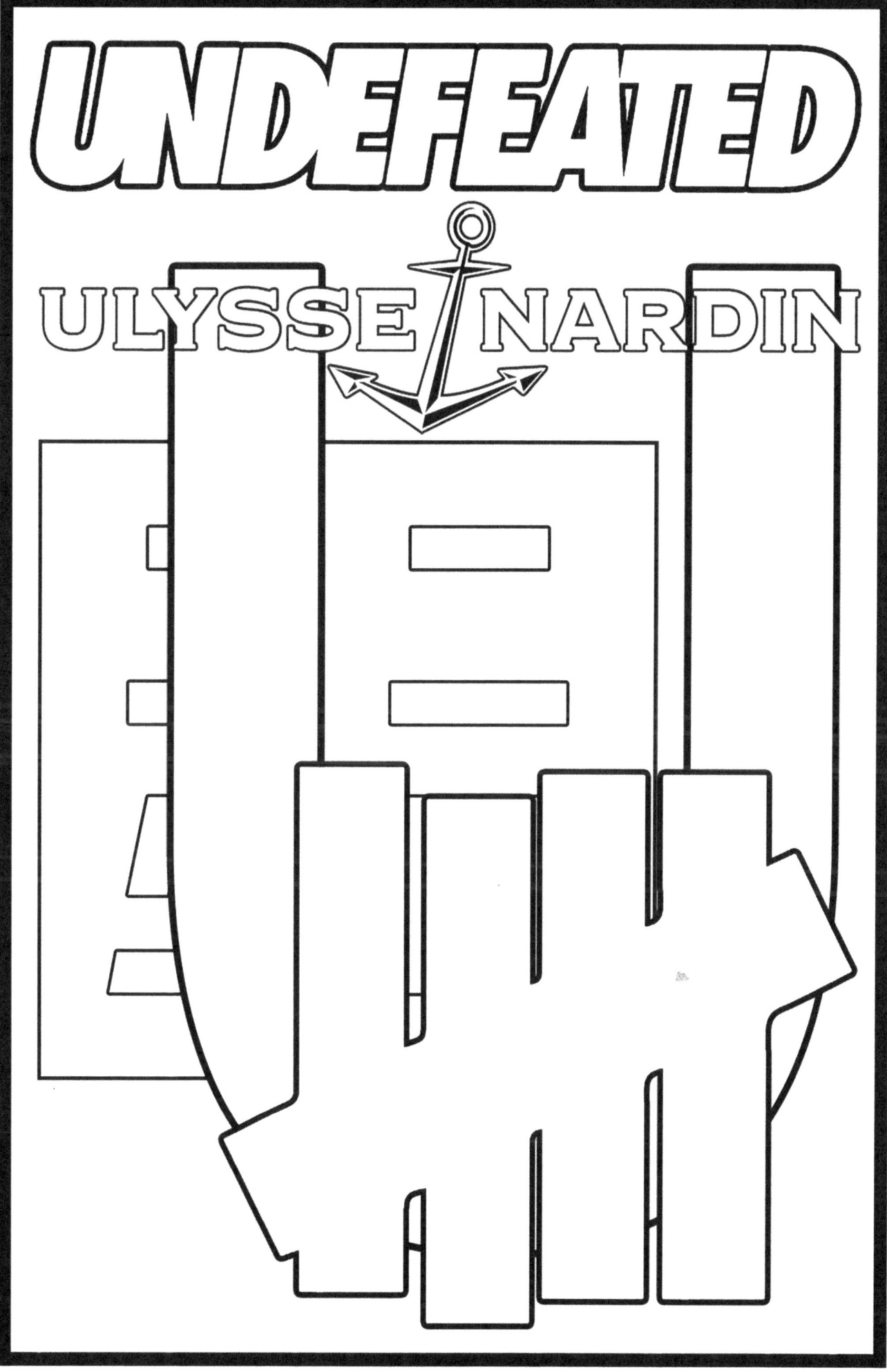

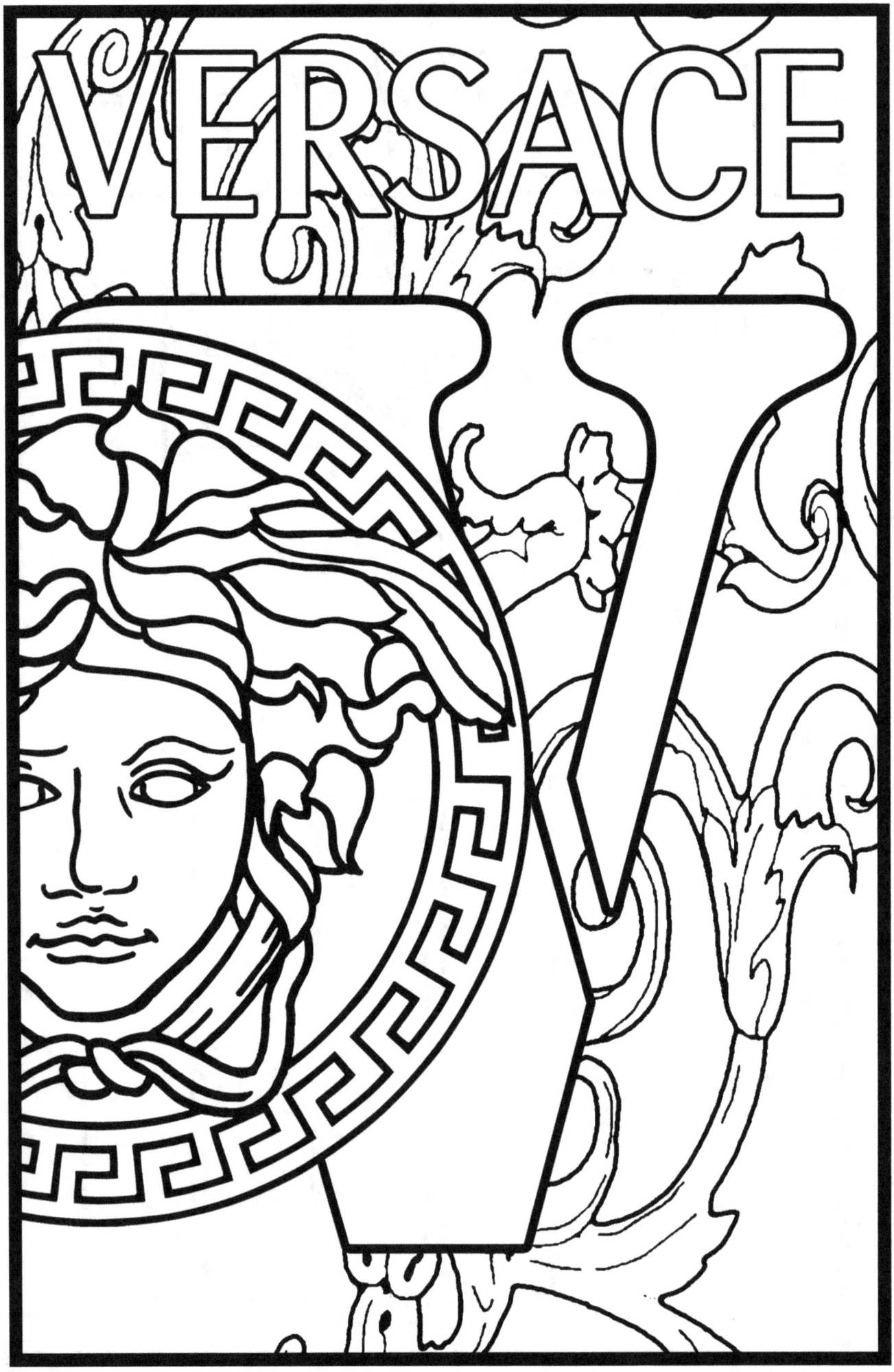

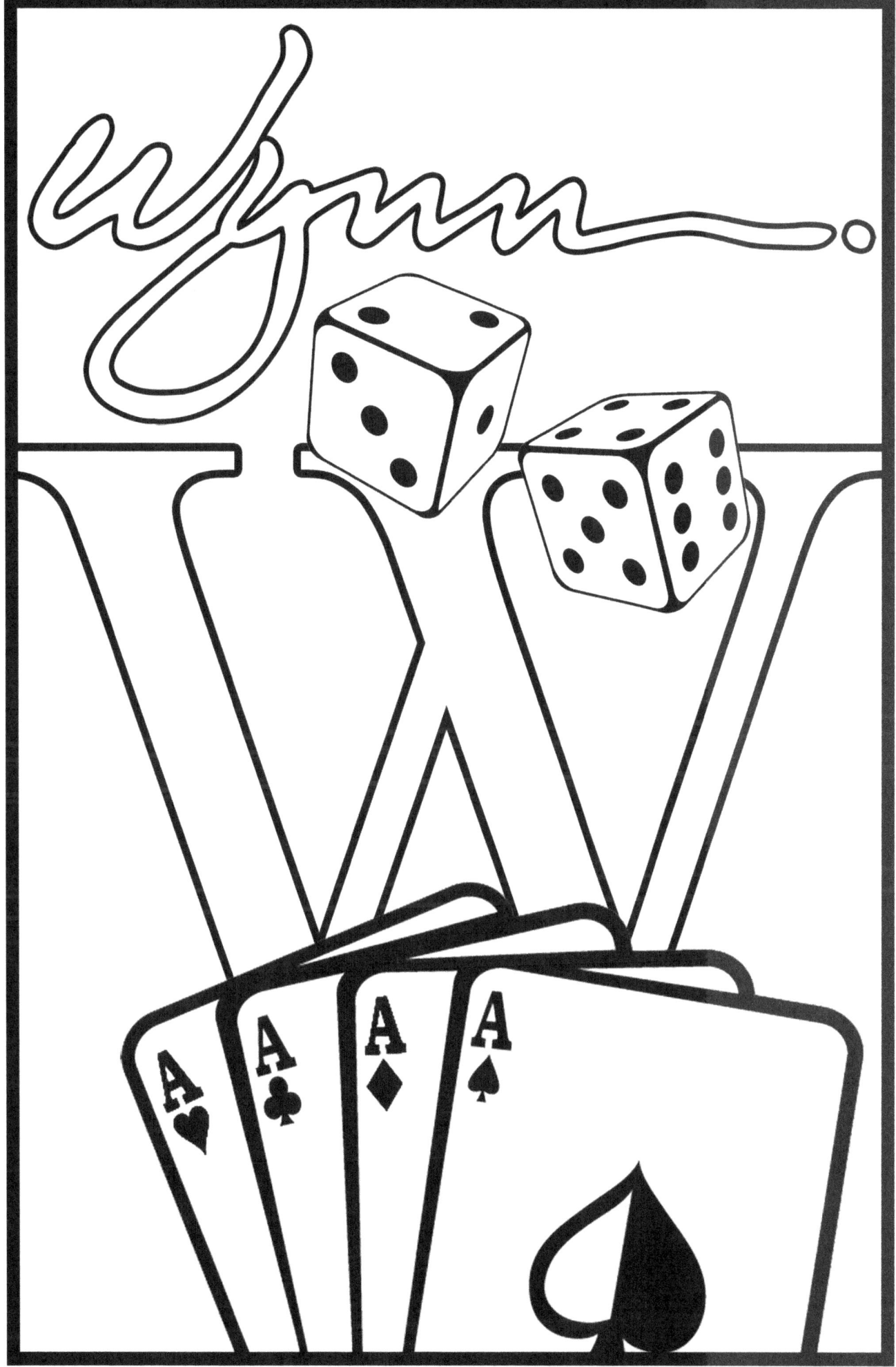

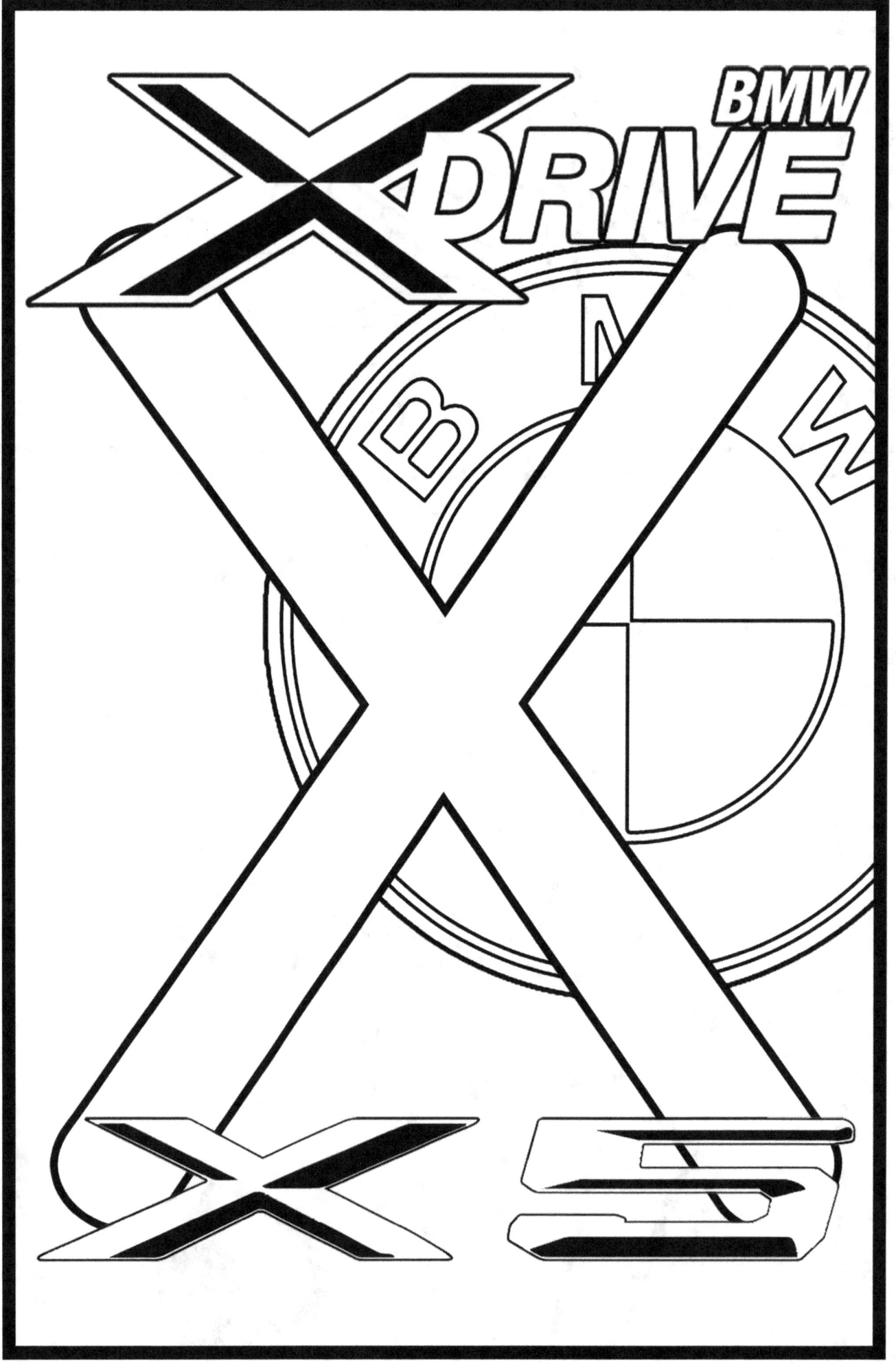

YOHJI YAMAMOTO

YVES SAINT LAURENT

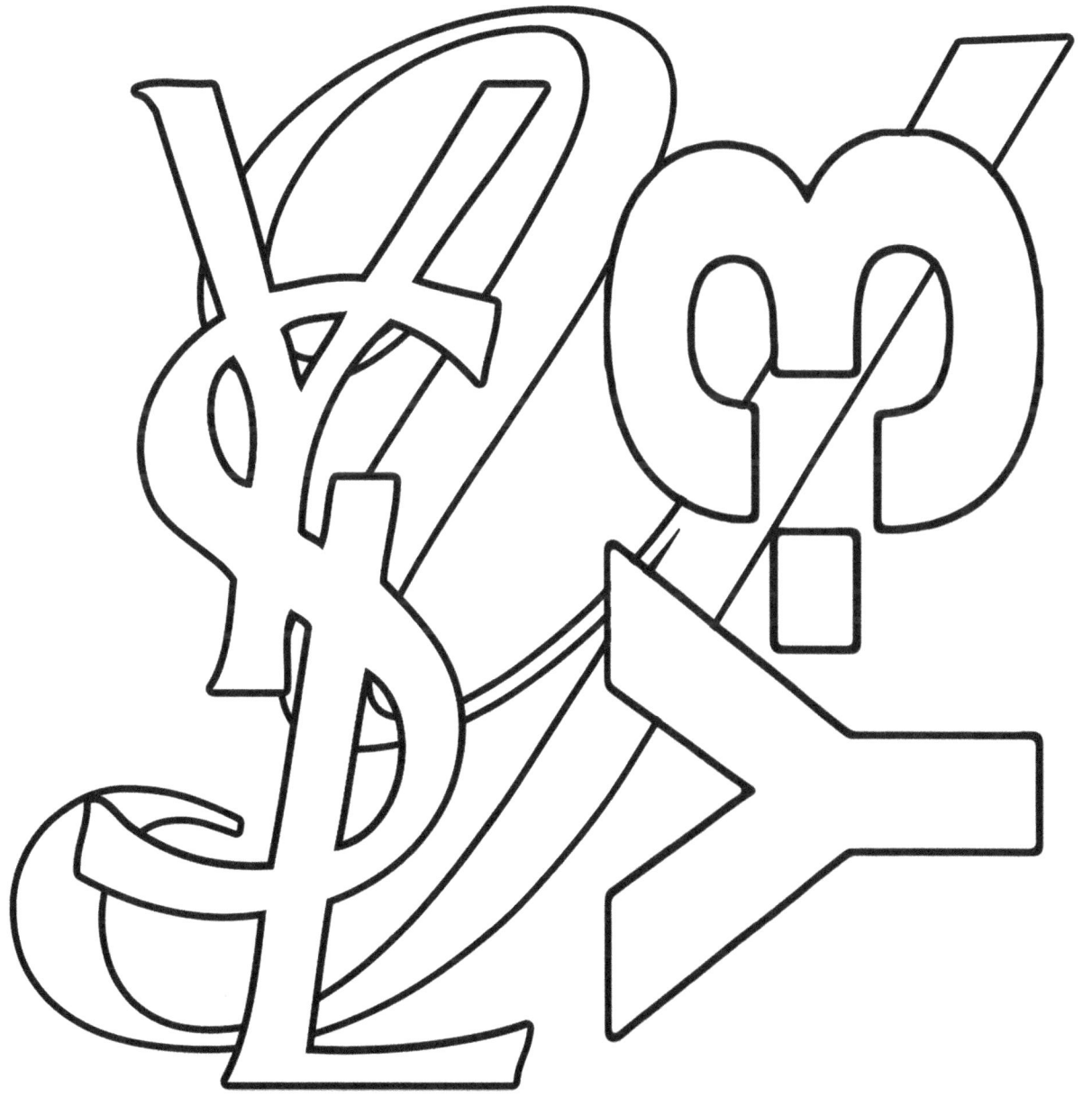

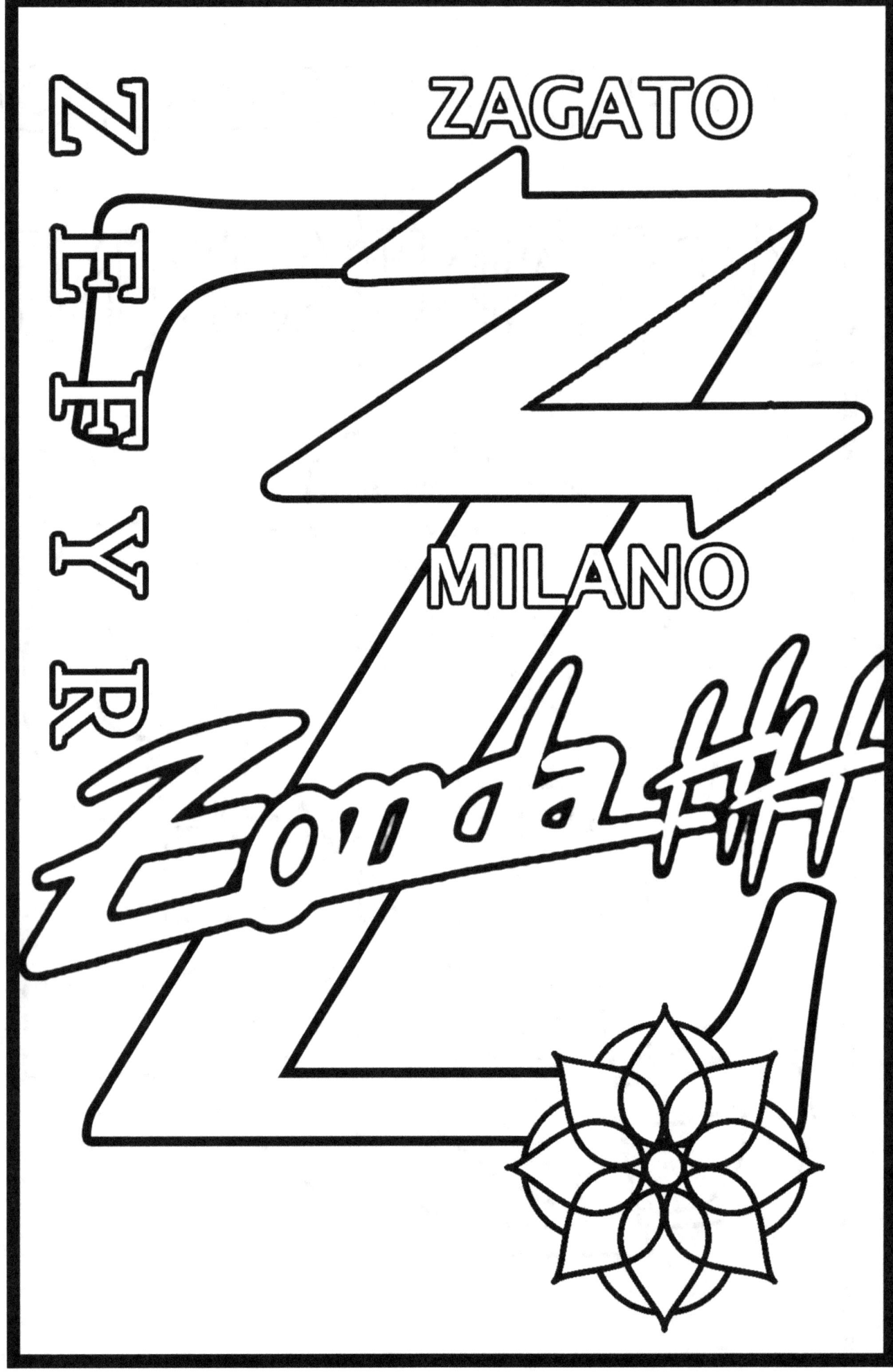